Sleepyheads Christmas Story

Alan and Linda Parry

Ages 4-7

Christmas

A Faith Parenting Guide can be found on the back cover

www.cookcommunications.com/kidz

"It's no good!" said Sig. "I can't get to sleep!"

"Neither can we!" said Tic and Fifi, the Sleepyhead twins.

And Dot, who was the youngest Sleepyhead Bear, was wide awake, too.

It was late Christmas Eve and the little Sleepyhead Bears were just too excited to sleep.

"I keep wondering what Mum and Dad have bought us for Christmas!" said Sig.

"So do I!" said Fifi.

"I've got an idea!" cried Sig. "Let's try to find our presents!"

"Yes, let's," said Dot.

"But we must be quiet," said Fifi. "If Mum and Dad wake up we'll be in trouble!"

So the Sleepyhead Bears began to search for their presents. First, they climbed up onto the big wardrobe on the landing. They found an old box of Christmas decorations. But their presents were not there.

Then the Sleepyhead Bears tiptoed down stairs and crept into the kitchen.

They found a huge Christmas turkey, an iced Christmas cake, and lots of mince pies. But they could not find their presents anywhere.

"Perhaps they are already under the Christmas tree," said Tic.

Chocolate mice and chocolate bells hung on the Christmas tree, but their presents were nowhere to be seen.

Suddenly, the door burst open and Mummy and Daddy Bear strode into the room!

"Now, what are all you children doing?" asked Mummy Bear. "You should be in bed asleep!"

"We can't sleep, Mum," said Sig. "We're too excited!"

"We can't wait to open our presents," said Fifi.

"Well, you won't get any presents unless you go to sleep," said Daddy Bear. "Father Christmas comes only to good little bears!"

At that, the little bears burst into tears.

"Well, what shall we do?" wept Tic,

"because we can't get to sleep!"

"I know," said Mummy Bear. "I will read you a

story and then perhaps you will be able to

settle down."

So the little bears sat on the big armchair with Mummy Bear while she read them a story.

It was such a lovely story that the bear children forgot all about searching for their presents and what they were getting for Christmas. Instead, they thought about the true meaning of Christmas.

"Thanks, Mum, for reminding us what Christmas is really about," said Fifi.

Mummy Bear cuddled her children close. It was snug and warm in her arms and soon the little bears fell fast asleep.

"At last!" said Daddy Bear, as he helped Mummy Bear put the sleeping children to bed.

Then, sometime later, when the moon was high in the sky, Father Christmas, who looked a lot like Daddy Bear, tiptoed into the little bears bedroom and filled four little stockings with lots of lovely bear-type presents.

The little Sleepyhead Bears had a great time on Christmas morning, opening their presents. They were very happy and excited all day; but they never forgot the wonderful, true story of Christmas that Mummy Bear had read to them on Christmas Eve, and it made their Christmas day even happier.